SORROW ARROW

OCTOPUS BOOKS

PORTLAND
DENVER
LINCOLN

EMILY KENDAL FREY

SORROW ARROW BY EMILY KENDAL FREY

COPYRIGHT © 2014 / ALL RIGHTS RESERVED

PUBLISHED BY OCTOPUS BOOKS / WWW.OCTOPUSBOOKS.NET

COVER ILLUSTRATION BY TREASURE FREY

DESIGNED BY DREW SCOTT SWENHAUGEN

DISTRIBUTED BY SMALL PRESS DISTRIBUTION / WWW.SPDBOOKS.ORG

ISBN 978-0-9851182-6-6

GRATEFUL THANKS TO THE EDITORS OF THE FOLLOWING PUBLICATIONS IN
WHICH MANY OF THESE POEMS FIRST APPEARED: *Aesthetix*, *H_NGM_N*, *Ink
Node*, *Interrupture*, *Jellyfish*, *LIT*, *Octopus*, *Pax Americana*, *Phoebe*, *Portland
Review*, *Rabbit Light Movies*, *Rattapallax* AND *Whiskey Island*.

Sorrow is the last fruit of youth.

RENÉ CHAR

SORROW ARROW

People are beautiful

Really stunning: necks, hips, cheek skin, pants

You are trying to walk to the store

You are only thinking about kissing

People are intriguing and boundaried

Tiny ships in paintings

A sandwich without several items

It hurts you to say that

You go home and give away all of your books

Gorgeous, articulated people

Moving into their names

Not having money is real

Big mean crow in a tree

Your body image in the distance is the image

Love is a mesh handbag

Love on the asphalt

We're shaking—blurry, almost

The suffering of us

At the center of suffering is love

The Greeks sank

Their bodies gold

My body is Greek

What can I say to you

Your dick inside someone

Night is a cloud

A big swathe of people

Darkness in the crevasses

Little earlobes

The green leaves already weeping

I feel Doric

I feel Ionic

My body thumps and rises

Curled symbol of ecstasy

I name myself Peninsula

Last night I tried to grow a comet tail

I flew around the living room visiting the dead

Spiders in lacy graves

My arms open as soft cheese

Milk chest

Wolf chest I heap my limbs on

I got so far in your pain that it rained

I hate you in your Batman shirt

The highway's river of heart-bits

People and their dream tigers

Sad as Whitney Houston

Someone stenciled a beet in three places on the overpass

I'm going to get a sandwich

The Telegraph Avenue part of me is

Why do you let your teeth sit on your lips that way

It's driving me crazy

Anyone with teeth and lips

I want to get on a horse and forget how to get off

You're going to notice the vase of yellow flowers

There's one picture from high school

Heart on a stick,

I want to sit in the car with you

The road in to the city is concrete tunnels

My brain sprayed on the walls

You would play pool and the shiny husks of tattoos

I want to cut up photos of flags

Send a stripe to you

You are stringing arrows by a lilac bush

Every time I forget a person my body apologizes

Bad night of dreaming

The rows of devils thick as trash

I want a world I can get inside

We cross the street

In our bone marrow is bread

An iguana came out of my dream hole

Every day I lose the thing and put it back where I found it

I used to be so there under a tree

I really felt I was interested in freedom

Mother of death talk

Mother of my fear of death

Don't fuck with me, Christian PTA moms

My sandwich is overly mayonnaised

The cheapest thing to do in winter is get a disease

No one can figure out where the sky comes from

Trees lifting into the mist

The horrible light of morning

Shuffle in and out of sleep

Thighs aching like a giant

Moms twisting their fingers on Caesar salad napkins

Moms with empathic bangs

Pin a badge on the dirty river

With my god hand I put us inside my father's new heart

Out in the world there's another world hesitating

Woman with a visor

Man covered in puke

Baby eating milk

Out of me come barnacles

The sky shitting its soft hope

There are stretch marks on my past

Can I say that?

There's a person you see

On the beach

God or another stranger

You sit on a log

What's sadder than a car

At the beach

A car parked

I am absent from the Internet

Red heart responder

You enter

Someone else

A garden

My dad breathes

I sit by the strawberries

I'm a black tar wing of blackness

Can I list for you the games I'm bad at

Sign above the highway

A light

Every time we stop it moves

My badness evolves into another bird

Your self-hatred has lost its precision

A metal gleam pokes through

In my reverie we're eating boiled peanuts on barstools

It's not sexy to be at home with your things

While bulbous paper lanterns hang overhead

Girls, stop peeing on the seat

Close range snowflakes

In my mind I'm running hard into your forehead

People are really useless when they're afraid

When I know you're making art I scream a little

My pants scream if you know what I mean

I feel so in love that I go to jury duty

I glide up the staircase

Looking for a way to be more you

Once my sister stopped eating

Small wagon

There was a place in the neighborhood called Silence-Heart-Nest

Sweet milky rice

Sometimes I walk so far for so long that the chalk in my mouth

   changes to metal

I make a baby and shoot it with my sorrow arrow

Hairs grow in patches along your jaw line

Radishes are fresh and tart

They look like fishcake

Later I'll buy a bike and ride out to a waterfall

When the world ends waterfalls will be the last to go

Piles of trash flowing beneath my legs

When I see fighting I wonder where babies come from

My childhood is full of wild strawberries

I dig holes for babies

I can't keep loving you if you won't take your sweatshirt off

You said In my opinion

Every garden is the same mossy green deepening

I saw you in your sweatshirt

Each night I get in bed with a fire-tongued aphid

So green and gauzy

We waterfall

The sidewalk is a rainbow taking me out of my life

There's an astounding amount of puke on city sidewalks

On weekends I invent errands so the birds won't know the real me

I come out over the mountains

When you loved me I was a flame in a boat

I called my grandmother but she didn't pick up

A stretch of silver trees

He's dead, I thought to myself, in bed

I got so sad I remembered being high in high school

How we pretended to be mummies, arms by our sides

Or chiefs of forgotten villages

Today I learned the word "earthmover"

Do you know what a bridge is

A picture exists of almost everything

In bed is where I realize people are dead

In our picture, my face grows wide as a teacup

The industrial revolution killed a lot of people

On the next big holiday I'll build a fort out of VHS versions of

   The Journey of Natty Gann

That wolf

She was always jumping from trains with her hair in a bob

If you're in love you have structure

Beams reaching over the shallows

That's what your eyes look like

That wolf

I sat next to a man on the shuttle bus

Alan? I said to him but it wasn't Alan

I kept reading the book

You don't want to think about the things I want to think about

No wonder bugs die

When I call an image to mind it's often your wrist and cheap watch

Tomorrow I'll march proudly into the day

Words streaming behind me and birds will want to shit

   on my shoulder

The sky will be lavender

It has no choice

Who are all of these people with guns and actual backgrounds?

I feel like an un-sent fax

When I feel like dying I go to bed

When I stick my hand in the death flower it holds

Turn off that music

You're glowing! they crow

I wish you didn't have so many small people on your face

I had to leave the café because of sexual tension

It was so loud

Yellow bee legs

There are a few styles of public readings

Women in flowy dresses

Taut verbiage

Slim males with deliberate facial hair

White people who think feelings are interesting

Breathing and breathy

Often a day ends upon waking

Why must you fiddle with time

What's this time bullshit

I want dilemmas involving god and coastal highways

The first person you loved will die

Their ass will be gone

All of your cats will die and their arrow jaws will break

Come with me

My mother was sad for ten years

The curtains will die

Your giant startling veracity

There's a greenhouse in the park next to the cemetery where Jimi Hendrix
is buried

Across the street is a big tree encircled with benches

Everyone will die

The wet smoke of night won't save us

You're so sad you're actually broccoli

In the art supplies store you touch the colored pencils

You're going to yell Motherfucking Asshole! at the next tree you see

Cut in half at the armpits

Glass of milk

We buy so many things, wooden world

A vise on your house

A vise on your motherfucking house

Once while camping I found some old people fucking

The woman wore a red swimsuit and her back was spotted

  like a baby fawn

Perspectives change based on the number of islands in sight

Some people will try to tell you what you mean

A cloud of gnats, for instance

This song I'm singing has ugly words

The movies are right

You know what you saw

What do people do at night

A pair of doves under an overpass

You walk to the corner

You eat a burrito

You conjure a woman and another woman behind her

You swallow and choke down shadows

In your guts is bitten off sunshine

Swollen and infested

It can't last much longer

You stood in the backyard with a bow and arrow

Your father hid from you in the lilac bush

He hid the moon from you

Even the planets laughed

There's a video of me crying

I was going to stream it live into your bedroom

But I couldn't find your bedroom

The distant cherries of my dreams

My sister on the blow up bed

Your voice, an ocean bell sounding

We used to call because we didn't know not to call

I used to keep calling into you because your body

You take the fan down to the basement

Summer is over

We used to be these people who hit at the sides

Now what

The dryer, the washer, the chair legs

I want to ride out over you like a boat with no legs

I'd like my shoulder to be your dominant archetype

Dads with babies in tiny baby hats

Regret screams from the vegetable stand

The science section infuriates

I dig babies from under strawberries

Everyone except for you is here with me

I'd like the green fuzzy seed I left on your desk

Atoms gather to massage my guilt

A direct path through the wilderness

Our inner snowmen

Die with me

I'm blazingly unremarkable

Face bunched like wet ham

I want to sit facing you and fall backwards off your lap

Marked so I come back less

Did you think there was room for "real" love

If you dug a hole in me you could get in

Wheel-y green trash container

I might grow large and contain your inability to contain me

You don't believe me

I am not believable because you don't believe me

In geometry we were given a protractor and a compass

It's like art the teacher said

I wore crayons to nubs filling space in

Rainbows taught me everything

You write the same dirge every day

You eat a snake

Grass grows around her and you light it

People run up to the heart bulb

Sometimes you want to come home

Wreath of black burned grass

I had a man like that

Every day I walked the pond just a ways from the overpass

Moving toward and within parallel lines

If I can just stay one current away

Glass of ice

Uselessly I entered him

We use people as paper cups

Write in pen

Make it sad so it won't come near again

My sister has planted a winter garden

At night the icebergs

Cartoon characters

Constantly dancing, I hope to save at least one of us

The sun sheds on her garden

Ridiculous music

Shaving halos in the air

I can see someone is failing

A great failure might occur

When I kissed the bundle

Of your mouth

Nothing came to the surface

That's how god works

Perched on your shoulder like a limp bird

I cried so hard I cried rice

It fell from my eyes

I'll love you later people sometimes say

Not now is a dynasty

Time stacks up then rises, steaming not-love

Eat it and love it

Hope is cabbage and rice

Death sweeps it away

We stopped at Runza

Eat this, you said, and I took a bite

Sometimes I want fewer choices

Asparagus or a baby with wings

You, returning with a bag of books

Another you, the green of your eyes watery astral bodies

Another me, less furiously edged

I waited by the back door

People moaned by, broke bottles

My father in the strawberries

Tattooing a reservoir on my chest

You do not love me

I knew it when I entered the duomo capped in mint green

    at the center of town

Jesus hung like a piece of toilet paper

Night opening its black flower

Every statue had bullet-sized holes in its feet

There are birds in the Madrid airport

Also, a lot of ham

I order cafe con leche

Strong? he asks me

Yes, strong, I say

Is anything funny anymore?

In Milan people had good eye contact

We found a glasses store

You look bad, he said, in those

Try this

I want to look smarter but I have near perfect vision

Europe has no children

No girls, anyway

A few boys eating sandwiches

I tried to have good posture as I slept

I know my mouth hung open a little

In Italy my sister is eating a digestive cracker

She's straightening her bangs

Her eyes

Her long-sleeved blue shirt

I'm sorry for the childhood we had to leave

I'd like to go back

Give her a drink of water

The Great Ones spent life on their knees

In the cafe next to the lilies

You breathe

The terrible sun begging

Love on a spear

You grow tall in your white t-shirt

A pigeon drags another pigeon to a tree

Eats

If I run over your arm will it feel like a pretzel

I give grief to the same structures on a daily basis

The lilies are reaching out their death

You keep trying to leave

We're lakeside on the same towel

This is the world one of us says

My grandfather nodding into his decaf

The car keeps going over the fence

The arm bleeds until love fills it

Our whole lives we're going to be metal towers rising out of
the wasteland

How long must we wait to be abandoned

Who reads books about gardening

You just put your hands in the dirt

It's not that I'm better but that my love is thicker

I disavow what I say when leaving the cavern

Remember my love letter

Burning like a planet in a drawer

Is anyone "ready" for anything

Readying, I stare at the ceiling from my crib

Blue velvet curtains

My father, singing

My mother in the garden, hopeful as a Marxist

Science is facts without value

Spectrometer of joy

In the park I gnaw grass

Man with spiked leather jacket taking self-portraits

It's arbitrary

If I let go, a burnished rainbow

Apparently I never finished my essay called The Value of Love

Three ferns outside your house, symmetrical and reaching

I loved you instantly

There's oil in the plankton that lines the ocean

On the fifth morning you rise, the air around you soft as islands

The white dog shits in the grass

You want your dream masts to rise

Oil covers the sloping lawn

The black dog eyes the roses

You want to put the cold egg of her breast in your mouth

Trash gilding the roadside bramble

You walk to the store

The first level of the food chain is contaminated

Giant rocks covered in oil

You sit in your body, quietly making blood

Wild blood

Bird of the world

Our rainbows faded

We'll grow old

Trends that back off

A light blue sweatshirt says WASHINGTON in puffy white letters

Plastic headbands that pinch at the spot behind your ears

A woman with a beautiful fishtail braid is pumping cream
    into her coffee

All night I dreamt of the possibility of dreaming

I woke to drink water, look out the window

Some sweatshirts are lined with a fake collar

You can still buy them at airports

People eating and eating and eating and eating and eating

I guess there's a point to it

Taking off their clothes, arm by arm

Leg by leg, getting into bed

The moon hurting itself on the sky

Waiting one day longer to die

At the airport bar people are drinking clear drinks

Your hands in cashews

The girl in gray shoes orders into the air

You're in love in your chair

Tethered so hard you make a groove in the landscape

You allow the god bird to gift you

You let the bird set fire, wetly flaming

Now the song on the radio is one from childhood

Something comes particle by particle through the air

Glowing curve of a small worm

Worm tail without a shell

You seek constantly the dying sticks of her body

You are breathing in your chair

Bathing in mustard seeds

The taped eyeglasses of sadness

A life without

The backyard birdbath

Moonlight on your back

The light not convincing you of anything

The bartender is dreaming

A way out of the seaweed cave

Later you'll say her name

Walk with her to the store

To buy cilantro

Afterwards you tell a story about a haircut

You stride out from our infinity

I watch the bird outside

I know a little about guns

You small your eyes

Language defeats prototype

You're going to do this and then this and also that

The novel I'm reading gives me hurricanes

Walls exploding and women with dead skin

Don't sing to me

I go back and move my hand from your leg

Leave the room

I leave the room so hard it burns a hole in the bed

The trees gnarl as you sleep

Orgasmic detritus

The woods become men

You wake to her face

Chicken salt sweat

The rain never stops

The planked sheets

She says "plum"

The rain is her and you touch it

The windows rowing you

Closer and/or farther away

Another article about bees dying off

Imagine fields of clover, unhumming

This morning the neighbor made his usual sounds

I made my own hole in the ecstasy

Berry muffin with a glazed top

Is that baby wearing make up

Throngs of strangers on the river banks

White cow, white bones, white chalk, white clay

The sun gives a confidence to his face

I twist my hair at the nape

There's a question we ask

About cowardice

You know the answer

French New Wave cinema is dead

You suspect you're not a person after all

Wars are citywide considerations

What if there was rubble

Your parents falling down around you

Your body throbs

Big-eyed flies

Your mouth on her arm

Piles to step over

She walks out into the field

Fingering the bright bones of her ancestors

What is music if not speech through sound

You hatch your future

You train a new dog to sit watch

You divide fear by delicate fear

Flies keep dying between my breasts

I walk you to the store and immediately you walk back

This is a mother-based problem

Stone buddhas carved into a mountain

Round the bend

If only we could back down from our obsessions

Make it inside and then out again

Don't die, summer

There are wolves among us

We promise to make more art

The second to last train stop overlooks a metal yard

A lot of people are eating

In the movie we're graceful, less monotonous

Not bunched up against the present

The sign at the church says heaven's got an edge

I don't want my donut

There's that picture book about the steam shovel that keeps digging

Old-fashioned nostalgia for a machine that works

My zone opens

I'll keep several appointments with a gaping zone

Then lob my machines into the cold swollen river

Some poets got married 20 hours after meeting

"Beauty will be convulsive or it will not be at all," he said

I should have taken you out to sea like Blackbeard

Let's walk through the mall and I'll buy you an Orange Julius

The day after we met one of my tiny succulents fell from the windowsill

I took a walk to a nearby mountain and breathed against the

   gates of a reservoir

Have you heard about the Hadron Collider

They smash particles together to find new matter

Once the machine got going so fast the currents blew out

With nowhere to go

I'm trying to believe in forgiveness

Under the earth's pink blanket is a set of ribs

Too big, even, for this

In Safeway I think things like:

The burning anus of my heart

and

Life is a battle-strewn battle

and

Your marvelous chest pump

On the walk home

My face puffed as a potato

I carry my unaddressed postcards

I pass the good dog

I touch his face

A radiation plume is making its way to us

We write it down so we won't think

Lap dogs sprinkled with acid snow

I got on the plane and sat back

Out the window I regretted complaining

I'm sorry I wasn't able to get inside your color

The sky was cobalt, deafening

I die so I can live

Outside category

You're immature

You go downtown

You exist on the top layer, stretching outward

Kombucha tea was taken off the market

Your mom walks the lake in the driving rain

Perhaps there's more

The sky is so demanding

In line at the grocery store benevolence descends

Man with thrice-washed spinach

You could be him

Now

With the coffin of love off you

You punch a hole in the subterranean

You go home

The neighbors' baby is out of town

They're fucking on the floor near the fireplace

It's spring

Called to the window, you sit by the window

Your skin suddenly moist

You put a baby inside her

Everyone's tethered

To the supermoon

On the drive to work I get a Greek feeling

Cherry blossoms punch the windshield

I miss you when it rains and outside of rain

The duplicitous gong of time

Your whole life you were afraid

Parents in the dining room

The mystery of plates

You close your eyes and walk down the beach

The ocean is quiet

Girl with cold-puffed ankles

I LOVE MY H

Sometimes her warm wing gets close to you

The ocean won't care what you kill

A bird eats a bird with its beak

When the tide come for us

You'll cry for your hands

Your hands like legs on her

It's too much

People with their falling down beauty

Their hats at angles

The woman DJ

You stand on some Cheetos

Nobody taught you anything but you kept expanding

Soft as plastic

Please don't be one of those people outside The 'Vern at 9 a.m.

Have a home

Sometimes do you pass a cemetery

And then a chair leg comes into view

A grove of trees

Same as memory

Sometimes I go on a walk

My unchosen legs

They move me

I was bent on you like a National Park

The question is always whether to be kind

To whom

It's raining like a bitchy teenager

Spit on the carpet

I want to be your mom a little

Scars on our foreheads

I name my god Get It Together

Your body is a fattening turd

A boat filled with hurt skeletons

A kind boat

Be the body you've abandoned

Stand in the water

The boat heavy and gone

The ocean eats its rocks

A house teeters on the precipice

Mean orgasm stuffed in bread

Give the birds their ocean

Delete the god document

You've got to get inside language to be free

A river runs hard down a mountain

You woke up and had been breathing

Love opens cliffside

An egg endlessly breaking

Dead flatscreen

You stand in time

Let me be shitty a little longer

The shine

Not even physics can prove existence

The body, escaping its yolk

Baby we are radically alive

In my car-boat I moan

In bed I stick my hand in and scream

A poisonous gas cruises the continent

Hand-clapping and euphonious

A warrior, I burn us

The moon's abuse

The moon, fat and hot

Fearless products of tenderness

My relationship to the unknown is in peril

A field of baking elephant shit

Love makes me permeable

The softest hurricane

Tiny computers are breaking into the clouds

Arrows are raining down

In line for breakfast I fuck the ground

I get inside the mailbox and bang around

Information equals empathy erosion

The more you know

You want the boy/girl splayed on the runway

The berry in your pocket melts

Hold still to let it bleed down your leg

You are unmoored

There's a word for it

In some countries they are napping

Waves hitting the shore

How did we get so naked

Out back there are rats in the compost

Egg shells and oranges

The neighborhood babies

We want not to suffer

We suffer for this want

Hour by hour

Piss and toilet paper

The mighty will not be felled by syllables

Sometimes I miss not one thing

The back of my throat a perfect road

With a new haircut

Your identity crisis got on the bus

I saw a barn in the distance

I had no intention

I wanted it to be our barn

I'm no more angelic than an albino pigeon

Made of French Fries

Made of park sex

Breasts a ʒ on the heaving scale

You want to get inside her laugh

She tips her head back

Her love used to be a horse

You kept your back to the field

Then one day you turned

Folded the flaps

A mountain rose like a lung in the distance

We are resurrected

At the store

There is light

Eggs break

People are driving long distances to have sex with each other

In the valleys

The birds

Hills burping their purple nipples

People are dangling in aestival light

Emerging, kissing mucus

We're sitting in the road with our fears fountaining

Pompadours of mud

Out of the backseat where we held each other

Unexpected, love

The imagined road

Our tiny childhoods

Mirrors of mud melting

We slip

We are closer to the mountain than we thought

In a Chinese prison they're tending my sex

I'm dreaming again

Fancy goldfish

They're building a ferris wheel over a bridge

The economy bursts

A giant eye

A neon apostrophe

Dumplings flowering in boiling water

I climb the Great Wall

In my pockets my wet hands

Love hangs, pre-eclampsic

Temple of Compassion

You are my enemy

I forgive you

Some people are making their way through the catastrophic jungle

List for me the ways again

An arsenal, our dream spatters

So much of nothing to be everything

I love her gray hair

Her delicate relationship to her jeans

People are making music and straining their chick necks into the rain

Crowned in muffin crust

Effete and tenderly sexless

Tiny mustaches

She looks in the mirror at her poppyseeds

She craves hot dogs

The loud and public advance of ignorance

I like her Chevy

I like her not yet extinct

She thrums in the sun

He is a body nearing hers

A continental wind

A tomato

An enormous protein moon

The not-love would hang

People aren't sorry

They take showers

Night is a cortex fissuring

Instruction manual for the reluctant father

I made up a joke about a didgeridoo

You were the only one

I could have told it to

Nothing accrues

I dream about you

You're naked making tablature for our future

Let's get in this sleeping bag

Dream cold

People think women are supposed to be friendly

Hey girl

A pie divided into pink slices

People don't know who they are

(Baseball)

When a woman talks

A few people listen

I'd like to suggest that when a woman talks we listen

Even though I have this giant problem in my pants

I am not going to do anything

Today the ocean

I am going to move my one sorrowless byte

London is overtaken with parakeets

Every park we never sat at

A plate of spicy octopus

A fight just for two

Ride the train with me

Be my

People are going to round the bases

Folds of hanging fat

I wanted something else to happen

Last night my mouthguard fell to the pillow, glowing and opaque

I yelled at your place in the sheets

What would it matter if I climbed up into the air

Made a bunk bed

Two-part breath

Like they taught me

In every rising graph is an eye

Looking beyond the page

It's hard to keep

The love in

Teach me to cook with green garlic

Who are we to stand in the path of God

You were eating beans late at night after

I was pure

The tight buds

A practicing narcissexual

A watermelon rind to be composted

I met you

The boat was built

Greed-soaked aluminum

Oh I cried and my beast snarled

Fear's mimesis

I shouldered arrows of sunlight

Strove with my beast at your extravagant darkness

Pale and cold

The back of your neck

We made up a word game

Love bloomed in cabbages

Time shook

Tender and rotting

You were eyeing my sister

You want to dominate her

She wants to be dominated

You give her back to the universe

You bring her home

God is the future of which we know nothing

Oily feathers

Nothing of lost babies

Horse skulls

The great grooved towers

Love of my life

Build me a crib

Animal me

A globular eye

Cracked in the nest

Stop throwing yourself on the horns of god

A paragraph built of complex thoughts

Go off grid

You never knew her

The ship can't reach harbor

Your mother in the hallway

Carrying a plaque

Your dad

Time steeps in the universe's milk

Stop farming downstream from shit

In the morning you pause

A succulent

You lick your lips

For this the collapse of love

You will meet a lot of people

Some of them will believe you

She is the pit

Tomorrow is judgment day

Rapture on my side

Deer on my hip

The lips of death

A hundred tangerines, rotting in a bowl

The hoopskirts of identity

Gold and breaking

You order a necklace

You order a porno

You're a porno inside a necklace on my neck

Ground out another tooth

We fall asleep

I climb the path

Bloody teeth rain down

It hurts to be born

God are you there

Are you standing in the shadow of my sorrow

Yet

INDEX OF *FIRST LINES*